Portrait Photography

9 Tips Your Camera Manual Didn't Tell You about Portrait Photography

James Carren

For more books by this author, please visit
www.photographybooks.us

Table of Contents

Introduction
Types of Portraiture

When confronted with the concept of portraiture, most people immediately cringe and think of the unflattering high school portraits. While a traditional portrait—and its offshoot, the headshot—are certainly one type of portraiture, there are a myriad other kinds as well. And a capable photographer can always create a graceful, traditional portrait.

Other types of portraits are: environmental, documentary, glamour and boudoir, fashion, lifestyle, conceptual, representational, abstract, and self-portraiture, among others. I'll explain a little bit about each type before we get started on learning how to take them.

A traditional portrait is typically taken using a simple three point lighting setup, with the focus on the face. It can be closely focused on the face, as long as the face is clear and sharp and does not become abstracted in any way. These are meant to be documentations of a person's appearance and are usually taken with the subject standing or sitting on a stool or chair. Personality can and should still be captured via the body language of the subject.

Environmental portraiture is next, and it's one of my favorites. It's sort of like documentary in that it's true to the life of your subject, but it can be more posed or more fluid. Here, the face is still important, but you want to make sure to capture the quirks of the environment as well. You're essentially making a statement about the person or people in the image via their environment. Environmental portraits can be done anywhere that is relevant to your subjects, from a job to an apartment to a place they frequent.

Documentary imagery is a little bit different from environmental portraiture. While environmental portraiture can be either posed or candid when the subject is aware of the photographer, a documentary subject may not be. If subjects are aware of the photographer, they've generally established a long-standing relationship, which allows their walls to come down. Also, in contrast to environmental portraiture which can be lit by extraneous lighting if necessary, documentary portraiture utilizes natural or available light. A documentary series may also include still-life or landscape photography as well.

Glamour shots are also generally referred to as beauty shots. The photo should give a representation of the subject, but the subject will be dressed up and in glamour makeup. It's a fantasy image, and accordingly, the lighting is often dramatic. Boudoir has a similar feel to a glamour shot, down to the makeup and dramatic lighting, but the emphasis is placed on sexiness and appeal, and can be shot either in lingerie or nude.

Fashion portraiture rides the line between a fashion shot and portrait. For example, a full-bodied fashion shot may not be considered a portrait because the photo emphasizes the clothes, not the girl in them. A fashion portrait is focused in at least to shoulder level and often advertises makeup or hairstyles. The fashion aspect is still present, and the photo may not be specifically about the girl, but her personality is much more evident.

A lifestyle portrait refers to the genre of portraits that includes engagement photos or family portraits in the park. The subjects decide how they want to look, and what kind of mood they want to capture, and the photographer creates it. It's the glossy, posed version of a truth.

Conceptual portraiture is my personal favorite and is generally how I work. It's explained in the name: the image is concept-driven and every item and pose within the image holds special importance. They can be taken in camera or constructed, and often are a combination of both elaborate sets and makeup. They can also be narrative in nature.

Representational and abstract portraiture veer the furthest away from traditional portraiture, in that they may not even contain a face in them at all. Representational portraiture is in fact, intentionally *not* a face. Instead, it may be a photograph that relates to the artist and some personal objects. For example, it could be a picture of toys from childhood, prospectively titled something like *Artist Age Five*. Abstract portraiture, in turn, may include sections of a face, such as eyes, lips or noses that have been cut out and rearranged. The image could also be intentionally blurred, made with a long exposure, or otherwise artistically rendered. Each choice made in regard to placement and color will have a specific meaning or theme for the artist.

Finally, we have the self-portrait, or the professional selfie. True to its name, it's taken by the artist of themselves, often using a tripod or handheld shutter release to help out.

I thought it was important to mention all of these types because the first chapter will address how to determine a personal aesthetic. In order to do this, you should have a thorough understanding of all the things that constitute a portrait. Regarding lighting, I'll only specifically address the more realistic types of portraits, although in the chapter about working post-production, I'll suggest techniques for creating conceptual or abstract portraits.

Chapter 1
Determining Your Aesthetic

The first thing to do before picking up your camera is to determine what type of portraiture you would like to take. The specifications for a shoot done with natural or available light will be completely different than the specifications for a studio shoot, or some combination of the two. I will address both in this book.

Once you've determined your type, think aesthetic. How would you like your image to look? Do you want it to be dramatic or natural? Airbrushed or true-to-life? Often with portraiture, it's good to already have these ideas in place so you'll know what equipment you'll need to make it happen. Sketch out your proposed lighting setup and decide whether you should also utilize tools, such as gels and flags, to create color casts or bounce light on your subject. Consider whether you need a seamless backdrop, and if so, whether it needs to be a half for a headshot, or a full for shooting the whole body.

A great way to get ideas, especially if you're new to the genre of portraiture photography, is to look at other photographers who you feel could be influential or important to you. Simply do a Google search, for example, of conceptual photographers. Also be sure to research reputable photography magazines, such as *Magnum*, *LightWork*, *Foam*, and *PhotoEye*. Bookmark artists that interest you and refer back to them if you feel stuck working in your chosen style.

It's always good, too, to have a working knowledge of the history of portraiture. Often, especially with conceptual or representational work, artists reference the styles and concepts of others. While this is perfectly permissible to do, it's good to know what artists you may potentially be referencing. It makes your understanding of structure, setup and concept that much stronger, because it has the power of understanding behind it.

It would be remiss of me to talk about the history of portraiture and not mention Julia Margaret Cameron, who was one of the first to step outside the box of traditional portraiture to create classically posed, conceptual character portraits. In addition, she often allowed her subjects to shift their positions as the exposure took place, causing a softness to her images that was not popular at the time.

Jumping a little under a century, it's important to note the presence of both George Hurrell and Edward Steichen, who popularized what we today know as Old Hollywood Glamour and/or Noir portraits. You know the image well: a beautifully coiffed young woman leaning into the light, coming from darkness.

Then there is Dina Goldstein, a contemporary conceptual photographer well-known for her elaborately constructed sets and controversial imagery, such as her Barbie series.

Doing research can inspire you to make more creative and informed work

Chapter 2
Establishing a Repertoire
with Your Subject

Often, when getting ready to do a portraiture session, amateur photographers will view it the same way that they would view shooting a landscape. But there is a huge difference, because as long as you don't litter, the environment is indifferent to your presence. People, on the other hand, work a little differently. Every single person, no matter who he is, will become immediately self-conscious when put in front of a lens, no matter the circumstance. This self-consciousness can manifest in many ways, from the model stiffening, to fidgeting or other quirks, or even to becoming a different person entirely from the one you set out to photograph. He might turn on another, sexier, or more confident persona, thinking that's what you want him to project.

In some cases, as in glamour and maybe boudoir photography, this other persona may be exactly what you want, but in most cases, it isn't. As the photographer, it's your job to break down any walls that your subject may have put up. In order to do this, you have to establish what I like to refer to as a working repertoire.

Let's start with regular old traditional portraiture. You want your subject to sit up straight, but you don't want him to look stiff. You also don't want him to fidget with their hands, which may cause movement in the frame. Even if you're old friends with your model, unless he has posed for you on several previous occasions, you have to consider that he will be nervous and/or behave differently because the dynamic has shifted. You, being behind the camera, are in control of the situation, whereas in your friendship, there is a more equal exchange of give and take. In order for you to get the naturalness you're looking for, it will be necessary to make him comfortable.

One strategy I like to use is to have my models come in before the shoot to get their makeup and hair done. That way, a conversation starts and you're able to have more of your typical friendship dynamic. You can also explain to your models what sort of shots you're looking for. When you get them in front of the camera itself, make sure that, while you're adjusting lighting and doing some test shots, you keep the conversation and the jokes flowing. This continuation will help keep them at ease. You may even be able to take several test shots without the models noticing. Granted, these will be what I call "in-between" shots, and unless you're really lucky, you won't get any usable ones from the test. Besides, luck is not what we want to concentrate on here. The point is, that by the time you start shooting for real, they won't be focusing on the camera as much.

If your models start getting nervous again, keep talking to them as you continue. Perhaps tell a funny story or give them encouragement or critique based on their modeling thus far. Reassure them that it's okay to feel like they look stupid, because they probably don't. If they are doing anything wrong, or not quite to your liking, correct them gently. This may even require you to go up and physically readjust them. Overall, throughout your session, keep the conversation and good energy going, and try to get a few natural smiles out of them.

Playing a soundtrack of music that fits the mood of your shoot can also be a natural way to get inhibitions to fall, and if your models are especially fidgety, it might be a good idea to ask them to get up and dance around and be silly. This will limber them up and make them laugh.

With both environmental and documentary portraiture, the demands on the photographer and subject are quite different. While in documentary portraiture, your subject doesn't necessarily have to know you're shooting them, environmental portraits are more posed, so this is necessary. And I believe, even with documentary, it's usually best that the subject know you're there. This way, you can begin, like in traditional portraiture, to build a relationship with your subject. It's going to be a little harder in this subset, though.

Typically, when you choose to do an environmental portrait or documentary series, your subject(s) will be people you've just met. Maybe they have a really interesting job, or a strong religious faith, or a lifestyle far removed from your own. Whatever it is that drew you to them, it's often not the best approach to just walk right up and say you want to photograph them. While some people will say yes, most will not, especially if you want to probe into a particularly private part of their lives. However, you can introduce yourself, express your interest, and begin getting to know them. The time it takes to gain trust can vary, depending on yourself and your subject. This is why documentary projects can take years, maybe decades. You have to have a lot of patience. After a while, approach the subject of taking photographs. Despite the trust you've built, they might be hesitant and need coaxing. Take your time; rushing could kill your project. On the other hand, they might be very open to it.

When you first begin photographing for environmental or documentary portraits, the situation with your subject will be similar to a regular studio shoot. She'll have some nerves, and may even get frustrated or angry with you for always shooting her, even though she agreed to the project. Push through this stage and keep going. After a while, this will wane, and she'll cease to even notice the camera. Again, this process takes a lot of time and dedication. It pays off though. Once you've gained this level of trust, you'll have the opportunity to take some of your most candid, truthful photos. It's up to you to be looking for them, however.

Chapter 3
Camera Settings

I would like to say here that in order to make a professional-looking portrait, you need to be using only semi-automatic or manual settings. You need to take a meter reading, and set your camera to a metering mode that will expose the background well, but place the emphasis on the subject. I would suggest either evaluative or partial mode.

After you've figured out your optimal aperture and shutter speed settings for the light you'll be working with, consider your method of shooting and your subject. If you're going to be shooting from a tripod, you can probably get away with a slower shutter speed or shallower depth of field. If you are shooting by hand, have your model stand in place and take a test shot to make sure there isn't any blur from camera shake. If there is, adjust your exposure to make your shutter speed faster. Program mode may be a good shooting mode to start with, since it will calculate proper exposure for you, and then you can just shift accordingly to remove any shake.

You'll also have to consider who your subject is. If you're shooting with an adult, you should be fine with a shutter speed that is only compensating for your own shake. If, however, you'll be shooting with a small child or baby as a model, you'll need to adjust your shutter speed to be very fast. This way, if they fidget, the camera can still capture a good, sharp portrait. If you are afraid that they'll bolt on you, you may also try setting your shooting mode to AI focus, which, while it won't change shutter speed, will automatically refocus if the distance between the camera and subject changes.

Chapter 4
Controlling Light Inside, Outside, and in the Studio

Good lighting is the key to everything you will do in photography, and it especially matters with portraiture. Your subject is the face, so the face is everything.

First, I'll talk a little bit about controlling light inside, working first with natural light, then available light, then a semi-studio setup. Second, I'll address how lighting can be manipulated while outside, and finally, I'll discuss traditional in-studio lighting setups.

Natural Light Indoors

Natural light is arguably the best and easiest kind of lighting to use, especially if you know how the light changes throughout the day. I have to say, though, that utilizing natural light for portraiture is a bit easier than with landscape. For one thing, you can utilize natural light indoors for portraiture.

"How do I do that?" you ask. It's simple: all you really need is a plain, solid colored wall or a five-foot seamless and a window directly facing it on the opposite side of the room. Preferably, the window should be north facing, as this will give you the most light and the most even light at any given time of day.

You'll have your subject seat themselves against the expanse of wall. Try shooting with them facing the window straight on, in profile, and at three-quarters. You should be getting fairly even, pleasing light, provided your exposure is set correctly.

Available Light

This section is all about utilizing the light available to you when you're indoors. It's a strategy mostly used in documentary photography. The genre is meant to be as true-to-life as possible with a subjective twist by the photographer. So, when you go to shoot a subject in his or her environment, you want to capture the aura of that place as truly as possible. Use your knowledge of natural light to help you. Available light is all about being observant and making use of sources around you.

The first thing to do is to open the curtains. Look for windows across from a place you may choose to shoot, such as a table your subject works at or a couch they like to sit on. If you don't have enough window light, look next for any lamps. You don't really want to use an overhead light, so make note of where the outlets are, and ask your subject if it's alright to move the lamps around once you have an idea of the places they frequent. It's even okay to replace light bulbs to make them brighter or dimmer. If you're still working with a lot of shadow, pay attention to how your subject moves around the space and intentionally compose your photos to make sure the light is nicely illuminating the face. This can create pleasingly dramatic photos.

Combination Available Light and Studio Light

For things like environmental portraiture, you could either be using available light or a combination of available light and studio equipment. Really, it all depends on the space you're going to be working in. If, for example, you're photographing a chef working in the kitchen, you don't want to get in the way of his job, and the kitchen may be too tiny or too busy for lighting equipment. In this case, you might just try a mounted flash paired with an external flash that fires just following the first to provide good fill light.

If you don't have an external flash to go along with your pop up flash, there is another technique you can use. Set your camera to program mode and a low ISO. Select evaluative metering mode, and then set up the flash. This combination should be able to provide enough fill to keep your photos from blowing out.

If you don't like the look that the flash gives, and you have the opportunity to bring in bigger lighting equipment, try using a simple three-point lighting setup to provide fill and rim light. I will discuss how to set up three-point lighting in the section on studio lighting shortly.

Outdoor Lighting

Yes, you can bring the studio lighting outdoors. But before we discuss bringing out the full array of lights and a power pack and generator, let's talk about some very simple things you can do to work outdoor lighting to your advantage. Firstly, use shade and don't shoot straight into the sun, as this can result in a blown out, hazy image. Face your model away from the sun so that the sun can act as a natural fill. Clouds can also function as natural diffuser if there are any. But your model's skin may still look a little flat or not have much glow to it.

To fix this issue, try using diffusers and reflectors. A diffuser is a white surface that will bounce light back onto your subject. You can buy one in flag form and have your assistant hold it close to or over your model. If you can't buy one, a sheet or white metal surface will work just as well. Note: a diffuser can also just be referred to as a white reflector. Other colors of reflectors will provide different effects. I have one that is five different colors in one: White, black, silver, gold, and bronze. If angled over the model's face properly, it can pop a subtle metallic sheen onto your model's cheekbones, or entire face. Black, unlike the other colors, will help to remove excess light from the face, and create more shadow.

If you choose to bring out the full lighting kit, here's what you'll need: A power pack, a generator to run it on, and two lights or less. At the least, a fill light, and at most, a fill and a hairlight. In order to make them less harsh, you'll want to use a soft box to diffuse your light. If you can't do all this, try just a light modifier on your external camera flash.

Studio Lighting

Now let's talk about the massive world of studio lighting. There is no way that I can cover everything in this short introduction to portraiture, but I will do my best to cover the basics.

The first thing I want to address is that, like with using natural light indoors to take a portrait, you'll need a nice wide open space with a white or plain wall and a facing window. Since you'll be completely manipulating the light in this case, fitting the windows with black curtains is a great idea. You'll also need a full size seamless (usually about six feet long) and some C-stands to hold them up. A C-stand is just a tall pole that can be adjusted, with a long rod in the middle onto which you will slide your seamless. That set up and taken care of, let's move on to the basic lighting equipment you'll need.

First, you'll need your power pack and flash kit. A power pack is a type of generator, and you're going to plug your lights into it so that it can control the flash mechanism of the lights. They'll go off in conjunction with the shutter. You can get an asymmetric power pack or a symmetric power pack. Asymmetric power packs split the light in the way you specify, meaning, for example, that one light can be supplied with seventy percent power and a second with thirty if need be. Symmetrical packs of course supply energy evenly. Given the choice, I would always choose an asymmetrical power pack, because they're more flexible. You can always set one simply to fifty-fifty. Having a pocket wizard is also useful, because you can change your settings on the remote and fire it off without having to touch the pack. That being said, you should always go over and discharge your power pack before and after a shoot.

Next, you'll need to get some lights. Hot lights should work just fine, and they come as a strobe with a reflector cover. You may also just want some plain strobes, with different kinds of reflectors. Make sure that no matter what kind of reflector heads you get, grids can be fitted onto them. Grids come in different spreads and shapes, with one of the most popular being a honeycomb. These can create interesting light and shadow affects. Definitely get a few, play around with them and see what you like.

Last on the equipment list is light modifiers. As discussed above, the reflectors that come on strobes, as well as honeycomb grids, are two types of light modifier. For certain lighting setups, you're also going to need: soft boxes, umbrellas, reflectors, gel filters, and barn doors, to name a few.

Soft boxes are some of my favorite tools. They come in a variety of sizes, and are fitted onto the light reflector. Soft boxes spread light more evenly and pleasingly over a subject. True to their name, they also soften harsh beams of light.

Umbrellas also serve to focus light by being fitted over top of your strobe or hot light. They capture the light and bounce it back onto the subject. Metallic reflectors can also be built into the underside of the umbrella, providing easy glow. Alternatively, you can have an assistant hold these at an angle to the model's face, as with the outdoor lighting setups.

Finally, stock up on all the little accouterments you can attach to your light. Here is a quick run down of some types that help you decide what you need, but I would suggest getting one or two of each of these and playing around with the different lighting situations they create. The world of studio lighting is so vast that it's very hard to learn much without doing and experimenting.

Barn doors, snoots and grids all help to focus light in different ways. Barn doors are exactly what the name denotes and can be closed down over your light to prevent unwanted spillage or to filter the light and only allow a bit to come through. It all depends on the level of opacity of your barn doors. Snoots are tiny, cone-shaped fixtures, and they help to create a narrow, focused beam of light. This can be good for lighting very specific details. Grids have been discussed.

Gels also affect light except that they don't direct light, they alter the color of that light. Gel packs typically come with a rainbow of colors that you can trim and clamp to your lights. You can also use multiple colors in one shoot, or different colors stacked over each other. If the color change appears very pale to your eye, don't worry. On camera, the color will come through as very concentrated.

The last piece of equipment you may want to consider is called Capture One. Capture One is a program that works in conjunction with Lightroom to allow you to tether your camera to the computer. Tethering simply means that the photo is going to go straight from the camera to the computer screen after you shoot it. This is great because you can immediately see on a full screen what the image looks like, whether it's sharp enough, and any other number of aesthetic considerations. If you don't like it, you can delete it immediately rather than doing it later, and if you do like it but it isn't exactly what you were looking for, you can use it as a reference to direct your model further. There are other programs aside from Capture One, although Capture One is industry standard.

Lighting Setups

Most lighting setups you'll need to figure out on your own via experimentation, and you can create a successful lighting setup using any number of lights. Lighting setups can be difficult, and with all the other logistics that go into planning a photo shoot, it's going to be very helpful to keep a lighting notebook. In it, I would record both of the basic lighting setups I'm about to discuss, as well as any experiments you do that you like. Keep a list of all the items you used to set it up, as well as any modifiers, and a number count of everything. Also, sketch out your lighting setup, even if it's just in stick figures. Describe how the lighting looks if you think you won't be able to recall it from the picture. This way, you have an easily accessible guide to refer back to.

Basic Two-Light Setup

For this lighting setup, which can work well for head shots and simple, less dramatic beauty shots, you only need two lights. These are your key light, or main light, and your hair light. You're going to place the hair light behind the model (of course out of the frame) and adjust the height so it's just above his or her head, illuminating the hair. This will help to separate the head from the background, especially if they are similar colors. You may need to soften the light so that a glowing halo doesn't appear around the head. You can do this by lowering the power on that light and/or by utilizing a soft box, just see which works best for your needs. Your second light, or key light goes just to one side of the camera, pointing at the subject, with about a five foot length of space between your model and the light.

Butterfly Lighting

Butterfly lighting is so-called because the arrangement of the lights creates a shape reminiscent of a butterfly on the model's face, via a shadow under the nose. This shadow is one of the few that is actually very flattering, as it makes cheekbones appear higher. It's often used in glamour or beauty shots. It will also help if your model has a weak chin. This lighting setup is very simple and only requires one light, positioned about five feet from the model, as with the basic setup. Place your light directly in front of the model and then raise it up a few feet, angling it downward to induce the shadow. If you feel that the shadow effect isn't strong enough, increase the power little by little until you are satisfied.

One Light

If you only have one light available to you, have no fear. You can still light your subject well enough to even out any shadows on the face that may be otherwise distracting. For this style, you have to be very careful not to create harsh shadows, especially if this light is your sole light source. However, to provide some fill light, you can utilize any window light accessible to you.

You're going to raise the light so that it's right above your model's head, angled downward towards his or her face. Tilt the light at a forty-five degree angle to his or her position. Turn your flash way down for this shot. If you're still finding the light to be too harsh, try either raising the light stand, or using a soft box to soften and even the light. You may also want to try this setup from both sides of the model to see which you prefer. The final effect should look very natural.

Rembrandt

You may be surprised to find that Rembrandt lighting, or lighting with lots of chiaroscuro (intense interplay of lights and darks) is very easy to do. Like all of the lighting setups above, it requires a maximum of two lights. One light is going to be placed on each side of the model. Put the light, as usual, about five feet away from the model, angled at forty-five degrees, and raised above the head at about six feet or more, depending on your model. The light on the other side should be closer, four feet or so from the model, approximately at eye level. Have the model pose so that the light falls dramatically across his or her face. The face should sort of appear to be emerging from the shadows. Use a reflector to pop a little light in there, as flash might be too harsh and create too much contrast.

Film Noir

Just for fun, I thought I'd throw in a little bit about my favorite cinematic style of lighting, film noir. Don't worry, you don't have to actually use film lights for this, although if you have access to them, go ahead. Film noir lighting isn't just a singular setup, as with a butterfly or Rembrandt setup. You can pull the style off with as little as two lights, although depending on how elaborate your setup is, you may use many more than that.

Essentially, noir just consists of a backlight and a key light. The backlight will be aimed at your backdrop or set, to dramatically illuminate it. As per usual, you'll want to place your key light so that it is in front or to the side of your model, angled downward, illuminating his or her face. You can also add multiple background lights, hairlights, or other lights to illuminate and create shadows on parts of your set.

Chapter 5
Focus on the Face, but Don't Forget the Pose

As we all know, basic portraits are about getting a good image of someone's face. You want it to be well-exposed, well-lit, smooth and flawless. But a lot of awkward portraits get made because, even though the photographer did a great job at capturing the model's personality and face, the body looks wrong. Often, this can happen because the photographer didn't pay attention to what was in the frame. Shooting from the shoulders up, you only really need to worry about the face, but from the waist up, you have to pay attention to the expression of the shoulders and hand,s too. No matter how relaxed someone's face may look, if his hands are clasped or clenched tightly, it's a dead giveaway that he doesn't feel comfortable.

This is also true of full body poses. If someone is modeling in a fashion shoot, for example, and she doesn't feel confident or is unsure of a pose, she won't go for it all the way, and the discomfort will show. This is part of the reason why Chapter 2 is so important. If you have your model's trust, she will feel less inhibited and be able to go all the way with poses and trying new things. You should also encourage her to do so.

However, no matter your model's comfort level, there are a few standard poses for each type of portraiture that can help you out.

Shoulders Up

I always try to start my test shots with the models sitting straight-backed, facing the camera. They can smile or not; whichever feels more natural is probably the best choice. You can also try a three-quarter or profile pose where they aren't looking directly into the camera. Variations of the typical straight on portrait are the over the shoulder look, and the hands on the face look, which are both big within the glamour genre. If you choose to do over the shoulder, treat it kind of like a three-quarter shot but with more of a twist. You want your model to swivel at the waist, not just turn her head like an owl, which both looks and feels uncomfortable. For hands on face, make sure your model has beautiful or interesting hands. If it's a beauty shot, you'll want to make sure that her hands are manicured and the nails painted beforehand.

Full Body

One way to get your model really comfortable and to ensure you get a natural pose is to have him sit as he normally would while holding a conversation with you. This will leave him engaged and show his personality.

Let's move on to laying or sitting poses. These can work really well for a lot of genres; they can be enticing for boudoir and sweet for something like a high school portrait; the difference depends on the expression in the eyes and the wardrobe. If appropriate, just have your model lie down, and try poses both on the stomach and back. You can create an easy, carefree atmosphere by having her fold her legs up behind her while on her stomach, or by putting her hands casually behind her head while lying on her back. You can create thousands of different poses just by differentiating the placement of hands or head, and the expression in the eyes. Be sure to give your model keywords to work with, moods you'd like to capture, such as *coy*, *flirty*, *happy* or *excitea*.

Standing poses work really well for fashion because they will display the whole outfit from head to toe. Try to start your model out in a very natural stance for him. Try having him move around the space, some with arms up above him head, some with hands casually in him pockets. Shoot from the front, side, and three-quarters as well as the back to see what he seems the most comfortable with and what looks the best compositionally.

If you're working with a particularly tricky model, here's a tactic to try: have them start out in a sitting pose on the floor. This will be the most casual and natural. While still down on the floor or other surface, have her move to laying poses if they work with the theme of your shoot. Next, have her move to a chair, and finally, you can have her in a standing position. Her body will be more limber and she should be less inhibited, especially if you need more sensual or sexy or irregular poses.

All in all, you just have to appear strong in your directing, and you will as long as you have some idea of the vibe and poses you want. Be firm and tell the model what you want. Both the model and the photographer should be experimenting and having fun.

Chapter 6
Shooting Self-Portraits

People take selfies all the time, and no matter what you think of them, the truth of the matter is that artists have been painting and shooting selfies, or self-portraits for as long as artists have existed. With the advent of smartphones that flip from outward shooting to self-portrait mode, it's easy to do. And with flippable displays on some cameras, it's easy to make sure that you've got yourself in focus. But what do you do if you can't see yourself? Taking a self-portrait suddenly becomes a whole lot harder, because it's up to you to compose, meter, focus, pose, and shoot.

Your two best friends in the art of self-portraiture are going to be your tripod, and your shutter release. A two-foot shutter release isn't going to help much though, so I would suggest either a wireless shutter release that you can conceal in your hand, or an air bulb shutter release that has a twenty-five-foot or longer cord, that you can hide under things like leaves, cloth or props. These are convenient because you can step on the shutter release, leaving your hands free to be expressive.

Now that you've got the things you need to help out, what about focusing? This, to me, is always the hardest part, because with metering you can typically use spot metering so that you are properly exposed. If the background is too dark or blown out, you can always do a second exposure that is correct for the background and combine them, or try evaluative metering mode and see if it works out better.

So, back to focusing. There's nothing more frustrating than thinking you've got your shot only to discover that it's blurry. Try using something else at the approximate distance away that you will be, and focus on that. It doesn't necessarily have to be as tall as you are, but if you want, you can use a light stand or a mannequin to be sure. Or, if you plan to be seated or leaning against a wall, tree, or other structure, focus on that in place of yourself. Once everything is in place, go and pose.

It's a little bit strange taking photos of yourself, so it may take you a few tries even if you've got all of your technical settings correct. To help yourself out, try applying some of the posing tips that I discussed in the previous chapter.

You may also need to play around with focal length, because unless you've got them memorized, you may find that you're zoomed too far one way or the other. This can affect your metering, focus and composition. Remember, a self-portrait can be as close in or as zoomed out as you want it to be.

If you still find yourself struggling, you may ask a friend to come along and look into the viewfinder. They won't take the photo for you, because you have the shutter release and you've set all your technical specifications, but they can tell you whether your composition, posing, and focus are good.

Remember, also, that self-portraits are generally a lot more personal than portraits you make of other people, and give yourself time to create a great one.

Chapter 7
Shooting Groups

Getting Ready

Shooting with one person is hard enough, so shooting with groups requires a bit of a different approach. Patience and confidence in taking control of the situation are going to be essential. The key here is timing, and the larger the group, the less time you can really take to get everything straight, because you'll lose attention quickly.

Let's start with smaller, more manageable groups, such as nuclear families, or engagement portraits, though the majority of these tips will also apply to larger groups, with some variation. Go to your location beforehand so you know what you'll be working with, and begin to plan where people should be standing. Also think about the poses you want people to be in; whether they will be sitting, standing, or leaning against anything or each other. It might be a good idea to do a preliminary sketch in order to help yourself visualize the photos.

Make sure you tell all of your models what time they need to be there, whether to pose or to get their hair and makeup done. If you have someone within the group who is a perpetual straggler, tell them a time that's earlier than you actually need in order to get them there on time. Unless the portrait is in some way conceptual, ask everyone to wear a solid color, although I would never suggest all the same color. When the people stand closely together, one solid color would look like a block with floating heads.

Tripod and Camera Settings

When everyone arrives, make sure that you're ready to go and that you have your camera mounted on a tripod to provide extra stability. Group shots are just not something you want to try and shoot by hand. You have to take control and tell everyone where to go, so that they trust you and follow your instructions. If you are fast and efficient, you'll be able to maintain control of the situation.

Before taking the photo, even just with two to four people, make sure everyone is ready. If you have them in a pose and need to make any sort of adjustment, make sure to specify, for example, whether they need to move a foot or just a tiny shuffle.

First things first, before you even take a shot, make sure all your camera settings are appropriate for what you're trying to do. Now is not the time to try and use a shallow depth of field, so pick a high f/stop. A fast shutter speed may also do you well, but that combination will of course depend on what exposure you need. It might also be a good idea to put your camera on AI servo mode, or a continuous shot mode, because once you've got everyone posed exactly how you want them, it's easier (and smarter) to just quickly take three or four shots before moving on to the next pose. This way, you have something to choose from, and in a situation like this, that's even more important than usual.

Posing

Now let's talk about organizing people. Obviously you want your poses to have some dynamic movement to them. To do this, you could try the traditional method of having some people stand and some kneel, et cetera, but a better idea if you need height variation might be to have people bring stools and chairs. And rather than choosing to arrange people with all the short people in front and tall in back, only do this for some of them. Also place some taller people toward the center of a group and shorter people along the sides for variation.

If you have a very large group of people, and/or they are all in very dynamic poses, you may want to shoot with a wide angle lens, or at least have one handy. Oftentimes in group shots, it's going to be hard to get everyone in the frame if they're too spread out. This means that people are going to need to touch one another, and in this case, whether the group is large or small, you should group people who have close relationships. In addition, having people hug or place hands on shoulders or scoop each other up is going to look a lot more natural and a lot less awkward than if they were all just standing in a straight line.

On Location

There are a few more specifications that should be taken into account if you're shooting on location instead of in a studio. Firstly, when selecting a location, make sure that it's large enough to accommodate everyone in the group. In some cases, you may have to get a little creative, but make it work to your advantage. If there are stairs or other elevated surfaces available to you, have some people get up on them and some stay down. This will also help to create the dynamism you need to keep the photo interesting. It will require you to get up higher as well, because you never want to shoot up when taking a portrait. No one wants to look up someone else's nose. Plus, shooting down gives you more opportunity to be creative.

Secondly, you'll want the location to have some importance to the people or scene you're photographing; otherwise, why bother choosing a location as opposed to the clean lines of a studio? If it's a conceptual shoot, consider the story you're trying to tell and pick the setting accordingly. If you're shooting a family, group of friends, or coworkers, pick a place that holds meaning for them or reflects their personalities. You may even want to ask about some suggestions they may have.

In studio, you don't have to worry about horizon lines, while on location you most certainly do. You never want people's heads to hit the horizon line; it's distracting. Make sure to look through your lens as you're composing your shot. What doesn't look like it will intersect to the naked eye may very well intersect in a photo.

Details

Finally, there are the details to consider. You may think that the larger your group picture, the less details have to be considered, but consider this: People spend a lot more time looking at group pictures than they do at non-group pictures. This is because they want to look for their friends and/or relatives within the group. So, you need to be paying attention to things like tangled jewelry, untied laces, flyaway hair and closed eyes. Obviously, some of these things are fixable in post production, but the more work you can do in camera, the better. You'll also want to tell everyone in the photo to tilt their chins upward just slightly, to avoid double chins and necks.

Post Production

Even though Chapter 8 is going to go into the details of retouching, I felt it necessary to mention that sometimes, no matter how many pictures of a group you take, not everyone in the photo is going to look great. This likelihood increases the larger the group gets. So when selecting your final image, you might have to composite several shots together to get exactly what you need. Pick the best base image with the fewest problems: good exposure, good highlight and shadow detail, good poses. Check out your other photos to fix those faces that might have closed eyes or motion blur.

Chapter 8
The Basics of Retouching

Basic retouching is actually very simple to do and doesn't involve any serious alteration of the features of a model. Rather, it involves making his or her natural beauty look the very best that it can. The things and amount you do to a portrait will differ with the age of the model, but the goal here is that you want the end result to look smooth and *almost* flawless, yet still real. Most of my instructions will apply to Photoshop, however, the Lightroom workflow will work very similarly for basic fixes, and I do have some tricks that I like better there.

General Workflow for Any Model

When you import your images into Lightroom or Photoshop, you'll need to do the basic corrections before any retouching can take place: correct the exposure if needed, bring up the highlights, make sure shadows are rich, and crop or straighten if your composition was a little bit off. I always recommend to try and do those fixes with the straighten tool before resorting to crop, because you lose image resolution by cropping. Also adjust dimensions and file type as needed so you don't forget later.

Non-Destructive Editing

In order to protect your original file and to get into the habit of non-destructive editing, make sure that you are either doing your spot correction on a copy of the original layer or on a blank layer. That way, if you mess up and don't notice it until you zoom out multiple clicks later, you can just zoom in, find the section that needs correcting, and erase it from the second layer, instead of starting completely from the top again. This isn't a tip for just the spot healing brush or even a suggestion. Non-destructive editing is something that absolutely has to be done in order to avoid a lot of heartache later. It's a lot easier to delete layers and work from there than to start over completely, and what's worse is that a lot of people who edit destructively don't even save original copies or jpegs, which puts them more than in a bind: they can never re-edit or fix the mistakes.

Teenage and Younger Adult Models

Teenagers have acne, and this is the first thing you'll have to remove before you can do any sort of skin smoothing. Luckily, this is fairly simple to do. Zoom in on your photo to about 300 percent, and select the spot healing brush tool. Make sure you adjust your brush for different sections of the acne, making the brush only as big as it has to be to remove the spot. This will ensure that the brush doesn't leave an obvious mark on the skin. Make sure, too, that your brush is sampling all layers, is content aware, and is set to zero percent hardness. Another trick I've learned in my time using the spot healing tool is that you cannot drag the brush across the area you're editing. This gets rid of blemishes quickly, but also leaves obvious evidence of editing. Instead, click repeatedly in the same spot to remove all of it.

Skin Smoothing

There are many many techniques that will successfully remove wrinkles and soften pores. I'm just going to talk about my favorite— and in my opinion, the easiest—option in Photoshop.

First, you'll make a copy of your image as retouched thus far. Grouping your layers by what sort of retouching you did is an easy way to keep everything easy to find. Also be sure to label each step as you go along so that you don't get confused. So, make a copy, and label it "skin smoothing." Go up to blend mode, and change it from normal to overly. Yes, it looks very strange, I know. Next, go up and apply the high pass filter. It's not in the filter gallery, but is down further in the menu under "other." Zoom in to your model's face and adjust the radius until you begin to see that all of her features are clearly defined. Don't overdo it; over-sharpening can make your photo look really fake. Be sure you're doing this on your copy layer, the same one you changed to overlay mode.

After this step your image will appear incredibly over sharpened, and you may be thinking, "How is this supposed to smooth my model's skin?" This is where the invert tool is handy, and will then make the high pass filter do the opposite of sharpen: soften. Of course, just as the image was over-sharp a minute ago, it will now be over-soft, and the softening will also be affecting parts of her face that it shouldn't. So, you're going to make use of the layer mask. Apply it to your high pass layer, and go over the model's eyes, lashes, lips, brows and hair to bring that texture back in. You may also want to bring in the skin texture just very lightly if the skin appears too smooth for you.

Removing Redness

Both younger and older models can have red skin blotches that makeup just won't cover. While you can try to use a spot healing tool and/or color matching tools, you may lose much of the skin texture you want to keep. The easiest way to fix blotchiness is to remove the red from the skin and then fix any skin roughness. To do this, create a hue/saturation layer. Again, you don't want to put alterations right onto your original. Select the red slider, and move it all the way up to full saturation. This way, you'll be able to very clearly see all of the reds in the photo, where they are in the skin, and thus, where you want to change the most. Use the bottom two sliders on hue/saturation (they kind of look like small black brackets) to narrow the focus so that only the reds in and around the face are affected. If you have a lot of bright reds elsewhere in the picture, they may also be affected, but don't worry: you can always bring them back in later using a layer mask. After you've got your focus area, drop the red saturation back down and watch all the blotchiness disappear. If you've still got a really pesky spot, you might need to also make use of the clone stamp and spot healing tools.

Chapter 9
Liquify Tool

Advanced manipulation is a very wide subject and I can't possibly cover it all. Like lighting skills, these different manipulations skills can take a long time and hours and hours of practice to learn.

One of the most popularly used retouching techniques involves slimming the model, whether just a little bit or extremely. The liquify tool is used to do this. The liquify tool distorts things, meaning that not only can it be used for slimming, but it could also potentially be used for things like conceptual portraits.

Liquify opens up its own dialog box of tools when you select it. These tools can be found in the upper, left-hand corner of the dialog box and from the top down are: the forward warp tool, the reconstruct tool, the pucker tool, the bloat tool, the push left tool, the hand tool and the zoom tool. When working on a specific section of the model's body, you'll want to zoom in and move using the hand tool to that section of the picture. Be sure to adjust the size and pressure of your brush tool as you go. I would recommend starting with a large brush size and working your way down to the smaller details, although you will probably need a smaller brush than you initially think even at the start.

If you check the box labeled Advanced Mode, you'll have access to a few more tools and some much more specific brush options. The extra tools are: the smooth tool, the twirl clockwise tool, and the freeze mask and thaw mask tools. You also have the capability to control your brush density and to add a mask to parts of your image if needed. All the tools are pretty self-explanatory, except at first glance, the freeze mask tool and thaw mask tool. All these tools do is make sure that a mask on your image is protected while you adjust other parts in liquify, and then gives you the capability to remove that protection when you're done or you need to work on another section.

When using the liquify tool, you will want to at least use a mouse, if not a tablet or syntiq, to give you added control, because the liquify tool takes an extremely light hand. This is really one of those tools that you just have to practice, so before you have a real shoot that requires this type of editing, you should pull up an old portrait and play around with it. Try making both airbrushed and surrealist looks with it.

Conclusion

You started out reading this small book because you wanted to learn a bit about the world of portraiture. Portraiture is one of the hardest genres of photography to master because it requires so much more from the photographer than does landscape or shooting objects. When you're dealing with people, you also have to work with their comfort levels and make sure that they understand exactly what is expected. You must at once become a people person and a patient leader, even if you're not.

Lighting is also really important, because while a landscape may be able to recover from so-so lighting, a face has so many nooks and crannies that light can make unflattering. Portraiture is also that much more expensive, because a lot of its sub-genres move you into the realm of studio lighting, and good quality equipment doesn't come cheap. Not only that, but it's going to take a lot of practice, patience and experimentation to learn everything there is to know about lighting setups. I do hope, however, that the few one- and two-light setups I've discussed are enough to get you started taking a solid portrait.

You've also got to learn to pose models, because unless you have the luxury of working with professionals, they won't know how to do it themselves, and even then, direction and communication are key. With practice you'll be able to handle not only one model but many, and after you've gotten a great shot, you have the skills to develop, edit and print it to whatever aesthetic you're trying to create.

Of course, practice makes perfect, so continue reading up on the art of portraiture photography. The only way you'll really learn and get your portraits to a professional quality, though, is to get in the studio and shoot!

Did you Like "Portrait Photography"?

Before you go, I'd like to say thank you so much for purchasing my book.

I know you could have picked from dozens of books on this subject, but you took a chance with mine, and I'm truly grateful for that.

So, once again, a big thanks for downloading this book and reading all the way to the end—I truly appreciate it.

Now I'd like to ask for a small favor if you don't mind:

Would you be so kind as to take a minute of your time and leave a review for this book on Amazon?

This feedback will help me continue to write the kind of books that help you get results. And if you loved it, then please feel free to let me know! :)